Count Your Wins:

Creating Momentum Toward Your Goals in Three Minutes of Reflection Per Day

Paula Engebretson

Count Your Wins: Creating Momentum Toward Your
Goals in Three Minutes of Reflection Per Day
by Paula Engebretson

Published by Paula Engebretson, LLC
Visit the author's website at
https://imbusybeingawesome.com

Copyright © 2022 Paula Engebretson

ISBN: 9798419024281 (print)
Printed in the United States of America
First Edition

Let's do this.

Why Count Wins?

"I wasted the entire day." "I didn't get enough done." "I'm not making any progress." Do any of these sentences sound familiar?

If so, you found the right journal.

It's time to recognize how much you do each day, how effectively you use your time, and the successes you regularly create; in three minutes per day, the prompts in this journal will help you do just that.

But why is this important? Why make time to recognize your wins?

First, making space for daily reflection activates the reward center in the brain and releases the feel-good hormone dopamine. Because this increase in dopamine creates such a pleasurable experience for the brain, it wants to keep generating more of these wins. (Hello, motivation!)

Secondly, recognizing wins helps build self-confidence. By continually identifying accomplishments each day, the brain begins rewiring its neural pathways and shifting its beliefs.

Rather than thinking, "I never accomplish enough," the brain starts realizing, "Wait a minute...I *am* a person who gets things done." "I *am* a person who uses their time well." "I *am* a person who follows through."

Finally, celebrating accomplishments each day provides your brain with compelling evidence of progress; by documenting your starting point and intentionally measuring your forward momentum, you highlight your growth. You see how far you've come. And you continue propelling yourself into action.

In short, with three minutes of reflection per day, you help fuel your motivation, self-confidence, and momentum toward your goals.

Are you in?

Let's go.

Count Your Wins

Where I'm At Today

Where am I right now, personally, professionally, and in my relationships?

_____

_____

_____

_____

_____

What are my wins from the past three months?

_____

_____

_____

_____

_____

What are my anticipated wins for the next three months?

_____

_____

_____

_____

_____

Where do I see myself one year from now, personally, professionally, and in my relationships?

_____

_____

_____

_____

_____

Where do I see myself three years from now, personally, professionally, and in my relationships?

_____

_____

_____

_____

_____

Today's three wins:

_____
_____
_____
_____

Tomorrow's projected wins:

_____
_____
_____
_____

Goals, thoughts, and ideas:

_____
_____
_____
_____
_____

. . . .

Today's three wins:

_____
_____
_____
_____

Tomorrow's projected wins:

_____
_____
_____
_____

Goals, thoughts, and ideas:

_____
_____
_____
_____
_____

Today's three wins:

_____

_____

_____

_____

Tomorrow's projected wins:

_____

_____

_____

_____

Goals, thoughts, and ideas:

_____

_____

_____

_____

_____

. . . .

Today's three wins:

_____

_____

_____

_____

Tomorrow's projected wins:

_____

_____

_____

_____

Goals, thoughts, and ideas:

_____

_____

_____

_____

_____

Today's three wins:

_____

_____

_____

_____

Tomorrow's projected wins:

_____

_____

_____

_____

Goals, thoughts, and ideas:

_____

_____

_____

_____

_____

. . . .

Today's three wins:

_____

_____

_____

_____

Tomorrow's projected wins:

_____

_____

_____

_____

Goals, thoughts, and ideas:

_____

_____

_____

_____

_____

Today's three wins:

_____

_____

_____

_____

Tomorrow's projected wins:

_____

_____

_____

_____

This week's wins:

_____

_____

_____

_____

_____

_____

My past self would be proud because:

_____

_____

_____

_____

_____

_____

Goals, thoughts, and ideas:

_____

_____

_____

_____

_____

_____

_____

Today's three wins:

_____

_____

_____

_____

Tomorrow's projected wins:

_____

_____

_____

_____

Goals, thoughts, and ideas:

_____

_____

_____

_____

_____

. . . .

Today's three wins:

_____

_____

_____

_____

Tomorrow's projected wins:

_____

_____

_____

_____

Goals, thoughts, and ideas:

_____

_____

_____

_____

_____

Today's three wins:

_____

_____

_____

_____

Tomorrow's projected wins:

_____

_____

_____

_____

Goals, thoughts, and ideas:

_____

_____

_____

_____

_____

· · · · · · · · ·

Today's three wins:

_____

_____

_____

_____

Tomorrow's projected wins:

_____

_____

_____

_____

Goals, thoughts, and ideas:

_____

_____

_____

_____

_____

Today's three wins:

_____

_____

_____

_____

Tomorrow's projected wins:

_____

_____

_____

_____

Goals, thoughts, and ideas:

_____

_____

_____

_____

_____

· · · · · · · · ·

Today's three wins:

_____

_____

_____

Tomorrow's projected wins:

_____

_____

_____

Goals, thoughts, and ideas:

_____

_____

_____

_____

Today's three wins:

_____

_____

_____

_____

Tomorrow's projected wins:

_____

_____

_____

_____

This week's wins:

_____

_____

_____

_____

_____

_____

My past self would be proud because:

_____

_____

_____

_____

_____

_____

Goals, thoughts, and ideas:

_____

_____

_____

_____

_____

_____

_____

Today's three wins:

_____

_____

_____

_____

Tomorrow's projected wins:

_____

_____

_____

_____

Goals, thoughts, and ideas:

_____

_____

_____

_____

_____

. . . .

Today's three wins:

_____

_____

_____

_____

Tomorrow's projected wins:

_____

_____

_____

_____

Goals, thoughts, and ideas:

_____

_____

_____

_____

_____

Today's three wins:

_____

_____

_____

_____

Tomorrow's projected wins:

_____

_____

_____

_____

Goals, thoughts, and ideas:

_____

_____

_____

_____

_____

. . . .

Today's three wins:

_____

_____

_____

_____

Tomorrow's projected wins:

_____

_____

_____

_____

Goals, thoughts, and ideas:

_____

_____

_____

_____

_____

Today's three wins:

_____

_____

_____

_____

Tomorrow's projected wins:

_____

_____

_____

_____

Goals, thoughts, and ideas:

_____

_____

_____

_____

_____

. . . .

Today's three wins:

_____

_____

_____

_____

Tomorrow's projected wins:

_____

_____

_____

_____

Goals, thoughts, and ideas:

_____

_____

_____

_____

_____

Today's three wins:

_____

_____

_____

_____

Tomorrow's projected wins:

_____

_____

_____

_____

This week's wins:

_____

_____

_____

_____

_____

_____

My past self would be proud because:

_____

_____

_____

_____

_____

_____

Goals, thoughts, and ideas:

_____

_____

_____

_____

_____

_____

_____

Today's three wins:

_____

_____

_____

_____

Tomorrow's projected wins:

_____

_____

_____

_____

Goals, thoughts, and ideas:

_____

_____

_____

_____

_____

. . . .

Today's three wins:

_____

_____

_____

_____

Tomorrow's projected wins:

_____

_____

_____

_____

Goals, thoughts, and ideas:

_____

_____

_____

_____

_____

Today's three wins:

_____

_____

_____

_____

Tomorrow's projected wins:

_____

_____

_____

_____

Goals, thoughts, and ideas:

_____

_____

_____

_____

_____

. . . .

Today's three wins:

_____

_____

_____

_____

Tomorrow's projected wins:

_____

_____

_____

_____

Goals, thoughts, and ideas:

_____

_____

_____

_____

_____

Today's three wins:

_____

_____

_____

_____

Tomorrow's projected wins:

_____

_____

_____

_____

Goals, thoughts, and ideas:

_____

_____

_____

_____

_____

. . . .

Today's three wins:

_____

_____

_____

_____

Tomorrow's projected wins:

_____

_____

_____

_____

Goals, thoughts, and ideas:

_____

_____

_____

_____

_____

Today's three wins:

_____

_____

_____

_____

Tomorrow's projected wins:

_____

_____

_____

_____

This week's wins:

_____

_____

_____

_____

_____

_____

My past self would be proud because:

_____

_____

_____

_____

_____

_____

Goals, thoughts, and ideas:

_____

_____

_____

_____

_____

_____

_____

_____

Today's three wins:

_____

_____

_____

_____

Tomorrow's projected wins:

_____

_____

_____

_____

Goals, thoughts, and ideas:

_____

_____

_____

_____

_____

. . . .

Today's three wins:

_____

_____

_____

Tomorrow's projected wins:

_____

_____

_____

Goals, thoughts, and ideas:

_____

_____

_____

_____

Today's three wins:

_____

_____

_____

_____

Tomorrow's projected wins:

_____

_____

_____

_____

Goals, thoughts, and ideas:

_____

_____

_____

_____

_____

. . . .

Today's three wins:

_____

_____

_____

_____

Tomorrow's projected wins:

_____

_____

_____

_____

Goals, thoughts, and ideas:

_____

_____

_____

_____

_____

Today's three wins:

_____

_____

_____

_____

Tomorrow's projected wins:

_____

_____

_____

_____

Goals, thoughts, and ideas:

_____

_____

_____

_____

_____

. . . .

Today's three wins:

_____

_____

_____

_____

Tomorrow's projected wins:

_____

_____

_____

_____

Goals, thoughts, and ideas:

_____

_____

_____

_____

_____

Today's three wins:

_____

_____

_____

_____

Tomorrow's projected wins:

_____

_____

_____

_____

This week's wins:

_____

_____

_____

_____

_____

_____

My past self would be proud because:

_____

_____

_____

_____

_____

_____

Goals, thoughts, and ideas:

_____

_____

_____

_____

_____

_____

_____

Today's three wins:

_____

_____

_____

_____

Tomorrow's projected wins:

_____

_____

_____

_____

Goals, thoughts, and ideas:

_____

_____

_____

_____

_____

. . . .

Today's three wins:

_____

_____

_____

_____

Tomorrow's projected wins:

_____

_____

_____

_____

Goals, thoughts, and ideas:

_____

_____

_____

_____

_____

Today's three wins:

_____

_____

_____

_____

Tomorrow's projected wins:

_____

_____

_____

_____

Goals, thoughts, and ideas:

_____

_____

_____

_____

_____

. . . .

Today's three wins:

_____

_____

_____

_____

Tomorrow's projected wins:

_____

_____

_____

_____

Goals, thoughts, and ideas:

_____

_____

_____

_____

_____

Today's three wins:

_____

_____

_____

_____

Tomorrow's projected wins:

_____

_____

_____

_____

Goals, thoughts, and ideas:

_____

_____

_____

_____

_____

·········

Today's three wins:

_____

_____

_____

_____

Tomorrow's projected wins:

_____

_____

_____

_____

Goals, thoughts, and ideas:

_____

_____

_____

_____

_____

Today's three wins:

_____

_____

_____

_____

Tomorrow's projected wins:

_____

_____

_____

_____

This week's wins:

_____

_____

_____

_____

_____

_____

My past self would be proud because:

_____

_____

_____

_____

_____

_____

Goals, thoughts, and ideas:

_____

_____

_____

_____

_____

_____

_____

Today's three wins:

_____

_____

_____

_____

Tomorrow's projected wins:

_____

_____

_____

_____

Goals, thoughts, and ideas:

_____

_____

_____

_____

_____

. . . .

Today's three wins:

_____

_____

_____

Tomorrow's projected wins:

_____

_____

_____

_____

Goals, thoughts, and ideas:

_____

_____

_____

_____

_____

Today's three wins:

_____

_____

_____

_____

Tomorrow's projected wins:

_____

_____

_____

_____

Goals, thoughts, and ideas:

_____

_____

_____

_____

_____

. . . .

Today's three wins:

_____

_____

_____

_____

Tomorrow's projected wins:

_____

_____

_____

_____

Goals, thoughts, and ideas:

_____

_____

_____

_____

_____

Today's three wins:

_____

_____

_____

_____

Tomorrow's projected wins:

_____

_____

_____

_____

Goals, thoughts, and ideas:

_____

_____

_____

_____

_____

. . . .

Today's three wins:

_____

_____

_____

_____

Tomorrow's projected wins:

_____

_____

_____

_____

Goals, thoughts, and ideas:

_____

_____

_____

_____

_____

Today's three wins:

_____

_____

_____

_____

Tomorrow's projected wins:

_____

_____

_____

_____

This week's wins:

_____

_____

_____

_____

_____

_____

My past self would be proud because:

_____

_____

_____

_____

_____

_____

Goals, thoughts, and ideas:

_____

_____

_____

_____

_____

_____

_____

Today's three wins:

_____

_____

_____

_____

Tomorrow's projected wins:

_____

_____

_____

_____

Goals, thoughts, and ideas:

_____

_____

_____

_____

_____

. . . .

Today's three wins:

_____

_____

_____

_____

Tomorrow's projected wins:

_____

_____

_____

_____

Goals, thoughts, and ideas:

_____

_____

_____

_____

Today's three wins:

_____

_____

_____

_____

Tomorrow's projected wins:

_____

_____

_____

_____

Goals, thoughts, and ideas:

_____

_____

_____

_____

_____

. . . .

Today's three wins:

_____

_____

_____

_____

Tomorrow's projected wins:

_____

_____

_____

_____

Goals, thoughts, and ideas:

_____

_____

_____

_____

_____

Today's three wins:

_____

_____

_____

_____

Tomorrow's projected wins:

_____

_____

_____

_____

Goals, thoughts, and ideas:

_____

_____

_____

_____

_____

·········

Today's three wins:

_____

_____

_____

_____

Tomorrow's projected wins:

_____

_____

_____

_____

Goals, thoughts, and ideas:

_____

_____

_____

_____

_____

Today's three wins:

_____

_____

_____

_____

Tomorrow's projected wins:

_____

_____

_____

_____

This week's wins:

_____

_____

_____

_____

_____

_____

My past self would be proud because:

_____

_____

_____

_____

_____

_____

Goals, thoughts, and ideas:

_____

_____

_____

_____

_____

_____

_____

_____

Today's three wins:

_____

_____

_____

_____

Tomorrow's projected wins:

_____

_____

_____

_____

Goals, thoughts, and ideas:

_____

_____

_____

_____

_____

. . . .

Today's three wins:

_____

_____

_____

Tomorrow's projected wins:

_____

_____

_____

_____

Goals, thoughts, and ideas:

_____

_____

_____

_____

_____

Today's three wins:

_____

_____

_____

_____

Tomorrow's projected wins:

_____

_____

_____

_____

Goals, thoughts, and ideas:

_____

_____

_____

_____

_____

. . . .

Today's three wins:

_____

_____

_____

_____

Tomorrow's projected wins:

_____

_____

_____

_____

Goals, thoughts, and ideas:

_____

_____

_____

_____

_____

Today's three wins:

_____

_____

_____

_____

Tomorrow's projected wins:

_____

_____

_____

_____

Goals, thoughts, and ideas:

_____

_____

_____

_____

_____

. . . .

Today's three wins:

_____

_____

_____

_____

Tomorrow's projected wins:

_____

_____

_____

_____

Goals, thoughts, and ideas:

_____

_____

_____

_____

_____

Today's three wins:

_____

_____

_____

_____

Tomorrow's projected wins:

_____

_____

_____

_____

This week's wins:

_____

_____

_____

_____

_____

_____

My past self would be proud because:

_____

_____

_____

_____

_____

_____

Goals, thoughts, and ideas:

_____

_____

_____

_____

_____

_____

_____

Today's three wins:

_____

_____

_____

_____

Tomorrow's projected wins:

_____

_____

_____

_____

Goals, thoughts, and ideas:

_____

_____

_____

_____

_____

. . . .

Today's three wins:

_____

_____

_____

_____

Tomorrow's projected wins:

_____

_____

_____

_____

Goals, thoughts, and ideas:

_____

_____

_____

_____

_____

Today's three wins:

_____

_____

_____

_____

Tomorrow's projected wins:

_____

_____

_____

_____

Goals, thoughts, and ideas:

_____

_____

_____

_____

_____

. . . .

Today's three wins:

_____

_____

_____

_____

Tomorrow's projected wins:

_____

_____

_____

_____

Goals, thoughts, and ideas:

_____

_____

_____

_____

_____

Today's three wins:

_____

_____

_____

_____

Tomorrow's projected wins:

_____

_____

_____

_____

Goals, thoughts, and ideas:

_____

_____

_____

_____

_____

. . . .

Today's three wins:

_____

_____

_____

_____

Tomorrow's projected wins:

_____

_____

_____

_____

Goals, thoughts, and ideas:

_____

_____

_____

_____

_____

Today's three wins:

_____

_____

_____

_____

Tomorrow's projected wins:

_____

_____

_____

_____

This week's wins:

_____

_____

_____

_____

_____

_____

My past self would be proud because:

_____

_____

_____

_____

_____

_____

Goals, thoughts, and ideas:

_____

_____

_____

_____

_____

_____

_____

Today's three wins:

_____

_____

_____

_____

Tomorrow's projected wins:

_____

_____

_____

_____

Goals, thoughts, and ideas:

_____

_____

_____

_____

_____

. . . .

Today's three wins:

_____

_____

_____

_____

Tomorrow's projected wins:

_____

_____

_____

_____

Goals, thoughts, and ideas:

_____

_____

_____

_____

_____

Today's three wins:

_____

_____

_____

_____

Tomorrow's projected wins:

_____

_____

_____

_____

Goals, thoughts, and ideas:

_____

_____

_____

_____

_____

. . . .

Today's three wins:

_____

_____

_____

_____

Tomorrow's projected wins:

_____

_____

_____

_____

Goals, thoughts, and ideas:

_____

_____

_____

_____

_____

Today's three wins:

_____

_____

_____

_____

Tomorrow's projected wins:

_____

_____

_____

_____

Goals, thoughts, and ideas:

_____

_____

_____

_____

_____

. . . .

Today's three wins:

_____

_____

_____

_____

Tomorrow's projected wins:

_____

_____

_____

_____

Goals, thoughts, and ideas:

_____

_____

_____

_____

_____

Today's three wins:

_____

_____

_____

_____

Tomorrow's projected wins:

_____

_____

_____

_____

This week's wins:

_____

_____

_____

_____

_____

_____

My past self would be proud because:

_____

_____

_____

_____

_____

_____

Goals, thoughts, and ideas:

_____

_____

_____

_____

_____

_____

_____

Today's three wins:

_____

_____

_____

_____

Tomorrow's projected wins:

_____

_____

_____

_____

Goals, thoughts, and ideas:

_____

_____

_____

_____

_____

. . . .

Today's three wins:

_____

_____

_____

_____

Tomorrow's projected wins:

_____

_____

_____

_____

Goals, thoughts, and ideas:

_____

_____

_____

_____

_____

Today's three wins:

_____

_____

_____

_____

Tomorrow's projected wins:

_____

_____

_____

_____

Goals, thoughts, and ideas:

_____

_____

_____

_____

_____

. . . .

Today's three wins:

_____

_____

_____

_____

Tomorrow's projected wins:

_____

_____

_____

_____

Goals, thoughts, and ideas:

_____

_____

_____

_____

_____

Today's three wins:

_____
_____
_____
_____

Tomorrow's projected wins:

_____
_____
_____
_____

Goals, thoughts, and ideas:

_____
_____
_____
_____
_____

. . . .

Today's three wins:

_____
_____
_____
_____

Tomorrow's projected wins:

_____
_____
_____
_____

Goals, thoughts, and ideas:

_____
_____
_____
_____
_____

Today's three wins:

_____

_____

_____

_____

Tomorrow's projected wins:

_____

_____

_____

_____

This week's wins:

_____

_____

_____

_____

_____

_____

My past self would be proud because:

_____

_____

_____

_____

_____

_____

Goals, thoughts, and ideas:

_____

_____

_____

_____

_____

_____

_____

Notes

Quarterly Check-In

Where am I right now, personally, professionally, and in my relationships?

_____

_____

_____

_____

_____

What are my wins from the past three months?

_____

_____

_____

_____

_____

What are my anticipated wins for the next three months?

_____

_____

_____

_____

_____

Where do I see myself one year from now, personally, professionally, and in my relationships?

_____

_____

_____

_____

_____

Where do I see myself three years from now, personally, professionally, and in my relationships?

_____

_____

_____

_____

_____

Today's three wins:

_____
_____
_____
_____

Tomorrow's projected wins:

_____
_____
_____
_____

Goals, thoughts, and ideas:

_____
_____
_____
_____
_____

. . . .

Today's three wins:

_____
_____
_____
_____

Tomorrow's projected wins:

_____
_____
_____
_____

Goals, thoughts, and ideas:

_____
_____
_____
_____
_____

Today's three wins:

_____

_____

_____

_____

Tomorrow's projected wins:

_____

_____

_____

_____

Goals, thoughts, and ideas:

_____

_____

_____

_____

_____

. . . .

Today's three wins:

_____

_____

_____

_____

Tomorrow's projected wins:

_____

_____

_____

_____

Goals, thoughts, and ideas:

_____

_____

_____

_____

_____

Today's three wins:

_____

_____

_____

_____

Tomorrow's projected wins:

_____

_____

_____

_____

Goals, thoughts, and ideas:

_____

_____

_____

_____

_____

. . . .

Today's three wins:

_____

_____

_____

_____

Tomorrow's projected wins:

_____

_____

_____

_____

Goals, thoughts, and ideas:

_____

_____

_____

_____

_____

Today's three wins:

_____

_____

_____

_____

Tomorrow's projected wins:

_____

_____

_____

_____

This week's wins:

_____

_____

_____

_____

_____

_____

My past self would be proud because:

_____

_____

_____

_____

_____

_____

Goals, thoughts, and ideas:

_____

_____

_____

_____

_____

_____

_____

Today's three wins:

_____

_____

_____

_____

Tomorrow's projected wins:

_____

_____

_____

_____

Goals, thoughts, and ideas:

_____

_____

_____

_____

_____

. . . .

Today's three wins:

_____

_____

_____

Tomorrow's projected wins:

_____

_____

_____

Goals, thoughts, and ideas:

_____

_____

_____

_____

Today's three wins:

_____

_____

_____

_____

Tomorrow's projected wins:

_____

_____

_____

_____

Goals, thoughts, and ideas:

_____

_____

_____

_____

_____

. . . .

Today's three wins:

_____

_____

_____

_____

Tomorrow's projected wins:

_____

_____

_____

_____

Goals, thoughts, and ideas:

_____

_____

_____

_____

_____

Today's three wins:

_____

_____

_____

_____

Tomorrow's projected wins:

_____

_____

_____

_____

Goals, thoughts, and ideas:

_____

_____

_____

_____

_____

. . . .

Today's three wins:

_____

_____

_____

_____

Tomorrow's projected wins:

_____

_____

_____

_____

Goals, thoughts, and ideas:

_____

_____

_____

_____

_____

Today's three wins:

_____

_____

_____

_____

Tomorrow's projected wins:

_____

_____

_____

_____

This week's wins:

_____

_____

_____

_____

_____

_____

My past self would be proud because:

_____

_____

_____

_____

_____

_____

Goals, thoughts, and ideas:

_____

_____

_____

_____

_____

_____

_____

Today's three wins:

_____

_____

_____

_____

Tomorrow's projected wins:

_____

_____

_____

_____

Goals, thoughts, and ideas:

_____

_____

_____

_____

_____

. . . .

Today's three wins:

_____

_____

_____

_____

Tomorrow's projected wins:

_____

_____

_____

_____

Goals, thoughts, and ideas:

_____

_____

_____

_____

_____

Today's three wins:

_____

_____

_____

_____

Tomorrow's projected wins:

_____

_____

_____

_____

Goals, thoughts, and ideas:

_____

_____

_____

_____

_____

. . . .

Today's three wins:

_____

_____

_____

_____

Tomorrow's projected wins:

_____

_____

_____

_____

Goals, thoughts, and ideas:

_____

_____

_____

_____

_____

Today's three wins:

_____

_____

_____

_____

Tomorrow's projected wins:

_____

_____

_____

_____

Goals, thoughts, and ideas:

_____

_____

_____

_____

_____

. . . .

Today's three wins:

_____

_____

_____

_____

Tomorrow's projected wins:

_____

_____

_____

_____

Goals, thoughts, and ideas:

_____

_____

_____

_____

_____

Today's three wins:

_____

_____

_____

_____

Tomorrow's projected wins:

_____

_____

_____

_____

This week's wins:

_____

_____

_____

_____

_____

_____

My past self would be proud because:

_____

_____

_____

_____

_____

_____

Goals, thoughts, and ideas:

_____

_____

_____

_____

_____

_____

_____

_____

Today's three wins:

_____

_____

_____

_____

Tomorrow's projected wins:

_____

_____

_____

_____

Goals, thoughts, and ideas:

_____

_____

_____

_____

_____

. . . .

Today's three wins:

_____

_____

_____

_____

Tomorrow's projected wins:

_____

_____

_____

_____

Goals, thoughts, and ideas:

_____

_____

_____

_____

_____

Today's three wins:

_____

_____

_____

_____

Tomorrow's projected wins:

_____

_____

_____

_____

Goals, thoughts, and ideas:

_____

_____

_____

_____

_____

. . . .

Today's three wins:

_____

_____

_____

_____

Tomorrow's projected wins:

_____

_____

_____

_____

Goals, thoughts, and ideas:

_____

_____

_____

_____

_____

Today's three wins:

_____

_____

_____

_____

Tomorrow's projected wins:

_____

_____

_____

_____

Goals, thoughts, and ideas:

_____

_____

_____

_____

_____

. . . .

Today's three wins:

_____

_____

_____

_____

Tomorrow's projected wins:

_____

_____

_____

_____

Goals, thoughts, and ideas:

_____

_____

_____

_____

_____

Today's three wins:

_____

_____

_____

_____

Tomorrow's projected wins:

_____

_____

_____

_____

This week's wins:

_____

_____

_____

_____

_____

_____

My past self would be proud because:

_____

_____

_____

_____

_____

_____

Goals, thoughts, and ideas:

_____

_____

_____

_____

_____

_____

_____

Today's three wins:

_____

_____

_____

_____

Tomorrow's projected wins:

_____

_____

_____

_____

Goals, thoughts, and ideas:

_____

_____

_____

_____

_____

. . . .

Today's three wins:

_____

_____

_____

Tomorrow's projected wins:

_____

_____

_____

Goals, thoughts, and ideas:

_____

_____

_____

_____

Today's three wins:

_____

_____

_____

_____

Tomorrow's projected wins:

_____

_____

_____

_____

Goals, thoughts, and ideas:

_____

_____

_____

_____

_____

. . . .

Today's three wins:

_____

_____

_____

_____

Tomorrow's projected wins:

_____

_____

_____

_____

Goals, thoughts, and ideas:

_____

_____

_____

_____

_____

Today's three wins:

_____

_____

_____

_____

Tomorrow's projected wins:

_____

_____

_____

_____

Goals, thoughts, and ideas:

_____

_____

_____

_____

_____

. . . .

Today's three wins:

_____

_____

_____

_____

Tomorrow's projected wins:

_____

_____

_____

_____

Goals, thoughts, and ideas:

_____

_____

_____

_____

_____

Today's three wins:

_____

_____

_____

_____

Tomorrow's projected wins:

_____

_____

_____

_____

This week's wins:

_____

_____

_____

_____

_____

_____

My past self would be proud because:

_____

_____

_____

_____

_____

_____

Goals, thoughts, and ideas:

_____

_____

_____

_____

_____

_____

_____

_____

Today's three wins:

_____

_____

_____

_____

Tomorrow's projected wins:

_____

_____

_____

_____

Goals, thoughts, and ideas:

_____

_____

_____

_____

_____

. . . .

Today's three wins:

_____

_____

_____

_____

Tomorrow's projected wins:

_____

_____

_____

_____

Goals, thoughts, and ideas:

_____

_____

_____

_____

_____

Today's three wins:

_____

_____

_____

_____

Tomorrow's projected wins:

_____

_____

_____

_____

Goals, thoughts, and ideas:

_____

_____

_____

_____

_____

. . . .

Today's three wins:

_____

_____

_____

_____

Tomorrow's projected wins:

_____

_____

_____

_____

Goals, thoughts, and ideas:

_____

_____

_____

_____

_____

Today's three wins:

_____

_____

_____

_____

Tomorrow's projected wins:

_____

_____

_____

_____

Goals, thoughts, and ideas:

_____

_____

_____

_____

_____

. . . .

Today's three wins:

_____

_____

_____

_____

Tomorrow's projected wins:

_____

_____

_____

_____

Goals, thoughts, and ideas:

_____

_____

_____

_____

_____

Today's three wins:

_____

_____

_____

_____

Tomorrow's projected wins:

_____

_____

_____

_____

This week's wins:

_____

_____

_____

_____

_____

_____

My past self would be proud because:

_____

_____

_____

_____

_____

_____

Goals, thoughts, and ideas:

_____

_____

_____

_____

_____

_____

_____

_____

Today's three wins:

_____

_____

_____

_____

Tomorrow's projected wins:

_____

_____

_____

_____

Goals, thoughts, and ideas:

_____

_____

_____

_____

_____

. . . .

Today's three wins:

_____

_____

_____

_____

Tomorrow's projected wins:

_____

_____

_____

_____

Goals, thoughts, and ideas:

_____

_____

_____

_____

_____

Today's three wins:

_____

_____

_____

_____

Tomorrow's projected wins:

_____

_____

_____

_____

Goals, thoughts, and ideas:

_____

_____

_____

_____

_____

. . . .

Today's three wins:

_____

_____

_____

_____

Tomorrow's projected wins:

_____

_____

_____

_____

Goals, thoughts, and ideas:

_____

_____

_____

_____

_____

Today's three wins:

_____

_____

_____

_____

Tomorrow's projected wins:

_____

_____

_____

_____

Goals, thoughts, and ideas:

_____

_____

_____

_____

_____

. . . .

Today's three wins:

_____

_____

_____

Tomorrow's projected wins:

_____

_____

_____

_____

Goals, thoughts, and ideas:

_____

_____

_____

_____

Today's three wins:

_____

_____

_____

_____

Tomorrow's projected wins:

_____

_____

_____

_____

This week's wins:

_____

_____

_____

_____

_____

_____

My past self would be proud because:

_____

_____

_____

_____

_____

_____

Goals, thoughts, and ideas:

_____

_____

_____

_____

_____

_____

_____

Today's three wins:

_____

_____

_____

_____

Tomorrow's projected wins:

_____

_____

_____

_____

Goals, thoughts, and ideas:

_____

_____

_____

_____

_____

. . . .

Today's three wins:

_____

_____

_____

_____

Tomorrow's projected wins:

_____

_____

_____

_____

Goals, thoughts, and ideas:

_____

_____

_____

_____

_____

Today's three wins:

_____

_____

_____

_____

Tomorrow's projected wins:

_____

_____

_____

_____

Goals, thoughts, and ideas:

_____

_____

_____

_____

_____

. . . .

Today's three wins:

_____

_____

_____

_____

Tomorrow's projected wins:

_____

_____

_____

_____

Goals, thoughts, and ideas:

_____

_____

_____

_____

_____

Today's three wins:

_____

_____

_____

_____

Tomorrow's projected wins:

_____

_____

_____

_____

Goals, thoughts, and ideas:

_____

_____

_____

_____

_____

. . . .

Today's three wins:

_____

_____

_____

_____

Tomorrow's projected wins:

_____

_____

_____

_____

Goals, thoughts, and ideas:

_____

_____

_____

_____

_____

Today's three wins:

_____

_____

_____

_____

Tomorrow's projected wins:

_____

_____

_____

_____

This week's wins:

_____

_____

_____

_____

_____

_____

My past self would be proud because:

_____

_____

_____

_____

_____

_____

Goals, thoughts, and ideas:

_____

_____

_____

_____

_____

_____

_____

_____

Today's three wins:

_____

_____

_____

_____

Tomorrow's projected wins:

_____

_____

_____

_____

Goals, thoughts, and ideas:

_____

_____

_____

_____

_____

. . . .

Today's three wins:

_____

_____

_____

_____

Tomorrow's projected wins:

_____

_____

_____

_____

Goals, thoughts, and ideas:

_____

_____

_____

_____

_____

Today's three wins:

_____

_____

_____

_____

Tomorrow's projected wins:

_____

_____

_____

_____

Goals, thoughts, and ideas:

_____

_____

_____

_____

_____

. . . .

Today's three wins:

_____

_____

_____

_____

Tomorrow's projected wins:

_____

_____

_____

_____

Goals, thoughts, and ideas:

_____

_____

_____

_____

_____

Today's three wins:

_____

_____

_____

_____

Tomorrow's projected wins:

_____

_____

_____

_____

Goals, thoughts, and ideas:

_____

_____

_____

_____

_____

. . . .

Today's three wins:

_____

_____

_____

_____

Tomorrow's projected wins:

_____

_____

_____

_____

Goals, thoughts, and ideas:

_____

_____

_____

_____

_____

Today's three wins:

_____

_____

_____

_____

Tomorrow's projected wins:

_____

_____

_____

_____

This week's wins:

_____

_____

_____

_____

_____

_____

My past self would be proud because:

_____

_____

_____

_____

_____

_____

Goals, thoughts, and ideas:

_____

_____

_____

_____

_____

_____

_____

Today's three wins:

_____

_____

_____

_____

Tomorrow's projected wins:

_____

_____

_____

_____

Goals, thoughts, and ideas:

_____

_____

_____

_____

_____

. . . .

Today's three wins:

_____

_____

_____

_____

Tomorrow's projected wins:

_____

_____

_____

_____

Goals, thoughts, and ideas:

_____

_____

_____

_____

_____

Today's three wins:

_____

_____

_____

_____

Tomorrow's projected wins:

_____

_____

_____

_____

Goals, thoughts, and ideas:

_____

_____

_____

_____

_____

. . . .

Today's three wins:

_____

_____

_____

_____

Tomorrow's projected wins:

_____

_____

_____

_____

Goals, thoughts, and ideas:

_____

_____

_____

_____

_____

Today's three wins:

_____

_____

_____

_____

Tomorrow's projected wins:

_____

_____

_____

_____

Goals, thoughts, and ideas:

_____

_____

_____

_____

_____

. . . .

Today's three wins:

_____

_____

_____

_____

Tomorrow's projected wins:

_____

_____

_____

_____

Goals, thoughts, and ideas:

_____

_____

_____

_____

_____

Today's three wins:

_____

_____

_____

_____

Tomorrow's projected wins:

_____

_____

_____

_____

This week's wins:

_____

_____

_____

_____

_____

_____

My past self would be proud because:

_____

_____

_____

_____

_____

_____

Goals, thoughts, and ideas:

_____

_____

_____

_____

_____

_____

_____

_____

Today's three wins:

_____

_____

_____

_____

Tomorrow's projected wins:

_____

_____

_____

_____

Goals, thoughts, and ideas:

_____

_____

_____

_____

_____

. . . .

Today's three wins:

_____

_____

_____

_____

Tomorrow's projected wins:

_____

_____

_____

_____

Goals, thoughts, and ideas:

_____

_____

_____

_____

_____

Today's three wins:

_____

_____

_____

_____

Tomorrow's projected wins:

_____

_____

_____

_____

Goals, thoughts, and ideas:

_____

_____

_____

_____

_____

. . . .

Today's three wins:

_____

_____

_____

_____

Tomorrow's projected wins:

_____

_____

_____

_____

Goals, thoughts, and ideas:

_____

_____

_____

_____

_____

Today's three wins:

_____

_____

_____

_____

Tomorrow's projected wins:

_____

_____

_____

_____

Goals, thoughts, and ideas:

_____

_____

_____

_____

_____

. . . .

Today's three wins:

_____

_____

_____

_____

Tomorrow's projected wins:

_____

_____

_____

_____

Goals, thoughts, and ideas:

_____

_____

_____

_____

_____

Today's three wins:

_____

_____

_____

_____

Tomorrow's projected wins:

_____

_____

_____

_____

This week's wins:

_____

_____

_____

_____

_____

_____

My past self would be proud because:

_____

_____

_____

_____

_____

_____

Goals, thoughts, and ideas:

_____

_____

_____

_____

_____

_____

_____

_____

Today's three wins:

_____

_____

_____

_____

Tomorrow's projected wins:

_____

_____

_____

_____

Goals, thoughts, and ideas:

_____

_____

_____

_____

_____

. . . .

Today's three wins:

_____

_____

_____

_____

Tomorrow's projected wins:

_____

_____

_____

_____

Goals, thoughts, and ideas:

_____

_____

_____

_____

_____

Today's three wins:

_____

_____

_____

_____

Tomorrow's projected wins:

_____

_____

_____

_____

Goals, thoughts, and ideas:

_____

_____

_____

_____

_____

. . . .

Today's three wins:

_____

_____

_____

Tomorrow's projected wins:

_____

_____

_____

Goals, thoughts, and ideas:

_____

_____

_____

_____

Today's three wins:

_____

_____

_____

_____

Tomorrow's projected wins:

_____

_____

_____

_____

Goals, thoughts, and ideas:

_____

_____

_____

_____

_____

. . . .

Today's three wins:

_____

_____

_____

_____

Tomorrow's projected wins:

_____

_____

_____

_____

Goals, thoughts, and ideas:

_____

_____

_____

_____

_____

Today's three wins:

_____

_____

_____

_____

Tomorrow's projected wins:

_____

_____

_____

_____

This week's wins:

_____

_____

_____

_____

_____

_____

My past self would be proud because:

_____

_____

_____

_____

_____

_____

Goals, thoughts, and ideas:

_____

_____

_____

_____

_____

_____

_____

Notes

_____

_____

_____

_____

_____

_____

_____

_____

_____

_____

_____

_____

_____

_____

_____

_____

_____

_____

_____

_____

_____

_____

_____

_____

_____

_____

_____

_____

_____

_____

_____

_____

_____

_____

_____

_____

_____

Are You Busy Being Awesome?

For additional strategies to help enhance your focus, boost your productivity, and design a life that works for you and your brain, tune into the I'm Busy Being Awesome podcast with Paula Engebretson at https://imbusybeingawesome.com.

Made in the USA
Columbia, SC
08 March 2022